Weekly Reader Books presents

THE BUG THAT LAID THE GOLDEN EGGS

by MILLICENT E. SELSAM

Photographs by Harold Krieger
Drawings by John Kaufmann
Designed by Lee Epstein

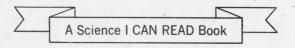

A Science I CAN READ Book

HARPER & ROW, PUBLISHERS • New York, Evanston, and London

To the mothers of the children who took part

This is a real story about real children.

I am the Millie in this story.

All of us tried together

to find out who laid

the golden eggs.

Millicent E. Selsam

MAURA NINA LISA BECKY

JERRY GREG MATTHEW BILLY ANNIE

There they were—all nine of them.

There was Maura.

There was Nina.

There was Lisa.

There was Becky.

There was Jerry.

There was Greg.

There was Matthew.

There was Billy.

There was Annie.

"Millie,"
they called.
Millie opened
the window.
"What is it?"
she asked.
"Could you
tell us
if we have
cricket eggs?"
asked Greg.

6

"Where are they?"
asked Millie.

"In the cricket
cage," said Greg.

"Where is
the cricket cage?"
asked Millie.

"In my house,"
said Greg.

"Well,
bring it here,"
said Millie.

7

In five minutes all nine were back.

They were pulling a wagon.

On the wagon was a large fish tank

with a cover on it.

"What a big tank for a cricket!"

said Millie.

"Do you have lots of crickets inside?"

"No," said Greg, "just one.

8

But we are going to catch more.

We like to hear them chirp.

We're going to have

a cricket orchestra."

"Where are the eggs?"

asked Millie.

Jerry opened the tank.

He took out a stem with leaves on it.

9

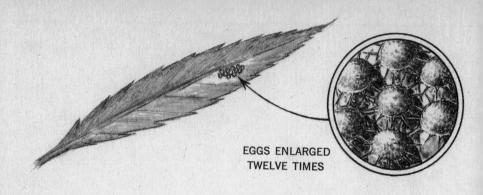

EGGS ENLARGED
TWELVE TIMES

"On this leaf," Jerry said.

Millie looked.

There was a little bunch of eggs

on the leaf.

They were gold and green.

"Are they cricket eggs?" asked Annie.

"I don't know," said Millie.

"But I have an insect book inside.

Follow me."

Everybody followed Millie inside.

She found the insect book.

She looked up crickets.

"It says these crickets

lay their eggs in the ground,"

she said.

"Then they are not cricket eggs,

because they are on a leaf,"

said Matthew.

"I wonder how they got into the tank,"

said Millie.

"You didn't have any other insects

in there, did you, Greg?"

"No," said Greg, "only a cricket."

"Maybe the eggs were on the leaf when

I put it in the tank," said Maura.

"That could be," said Billy.

"How can we find out what eggs

these are?" asked Becky.

"Let me see what the book says about

that," said Millie.

She got her insect book.

"Here it is.

The book says that if you know

what plant the eggs are laid on,

you have a good clue.

Let me see that plant."

"I know where I got it," cried Maura.

"I think it is a goldenrod."

"Do you think you could get

some more?" asked Millie.

Maura went out to look for the plant.

She came back with a goldenrod stem

in her hand.

"This is the bottom of the plant.

You can see where I cut off the top,"

she said.

"See if they fit together," said Billy.

Maura held the two stems together.

"They fit," she said.

14

"Now what?" asked Becky.

"The eggs were laid

on a goldenrod plant,"

said Millie.

"At least we know that much.

Let's get a good look

at the eggs."

She got a magnifying glass.

Everyone had a chance

to look at the eggs.

"They look empty," said Billy.

"Maybe they have already hatched,"

said Millie.

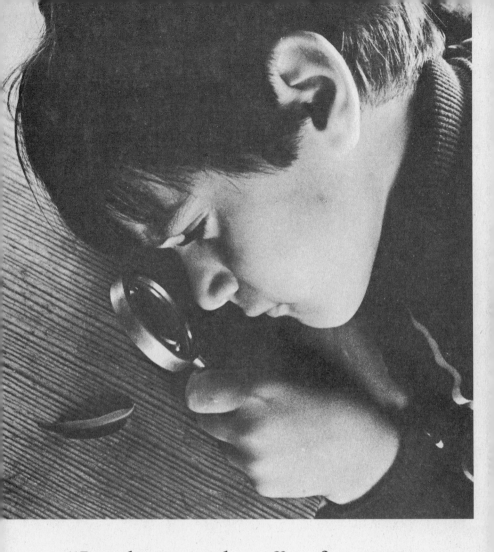

"Just let me take off a few eggs

and put them on a slide.

I'll look at them later

under the microscope."

"What shall we do now?" asked Nina.

"Let's write to the

natural history museum," said Lisa.

"They have a man there

who knows all about insects.

I took something to him once."

"What's his name?" asked Nina.

"You don't need the name,"

said Greg.

"Write to the Professor of Insects."

While everybody was helping

write the letter,

Greg's little brother, Ethan, came in.

"Can I see
the eggs?"
he asked.
"Yes,"
said Millie.
"Look at them
with the
magnifying
glass."

19

Soon the letter was finished.

This is what it said:

Dear Professor of Insects,

We found these eggs on a leaf in a cricket cage. First we thought that they were cricket eggs. Then we found out that these crickets lay eggs in the ground.

then we thought maybe
the eggs were on the
leaf before it was put
in the cage. we have
an insect book but it
does not tell about eggs.
the leaf was from a
goldenrod plant. Can
you tell us what kind
of eggs these are?

you will find them
on the leaf in the
envelope.
yours truly
Greg Annie Jerry Billy
Maura Lisa
Matthew
Becky Nina

Ocean Bay Park
Fire Island, N.Y.

Millie got up to get the leaf
with the eggs.

"Where is it?" she cried.

"It was right here."

"I bet Ethan took it," said Greg.

"When did he leave?" asked Millie.

"Ten minutes ago," said Annie.

"Let's look around here," said Millie.

All nine children and Millie looked.

They looked all over the floor.

There were no leaves.

And there were no eggs.

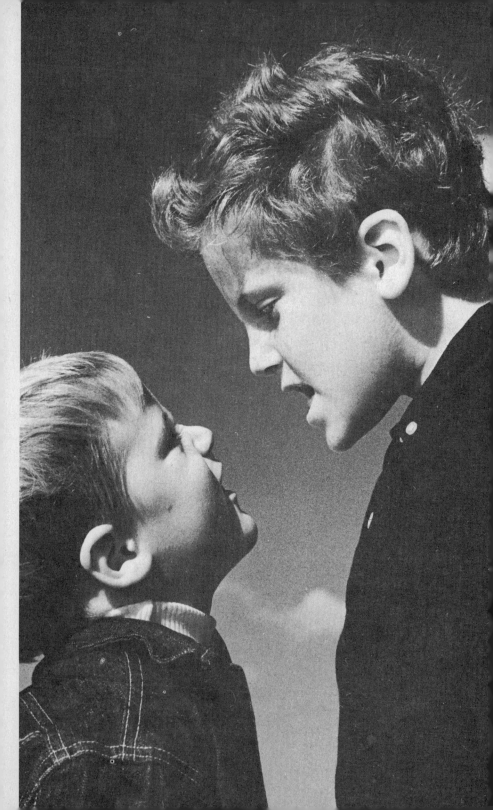

"Let's ask Ethan about them,"

said Matthew.

Everybody went out to look for Ethan.

"Here he is!" cried Greg.

"Did you take the leaf

with the eggs?"

"No!" said Ethan.

"Are you sure?" asked Millie.

"We need it to send to the museum."

"I did not take it," said Ethan.

25

"What can we do now?" asked Annie.

"You have a few eggs on the slide,"

said Becky. "Send them."

"No," said Millie.

"I'll save the slide.

When I go to the city,

I will take it to the museum myself."

"But meanwhile can't we

do something?" asked Billy.

"We can look for more eggs,"

said Maura.

"I guess that's what we have to do,"

Millie said.

"It's late now.
Let's meet tomorrow
at ten o'clock
near Maura's house."
"Why near
her house?"
asked Greg.
"Because I have
goldenrod plants
around my house,"
said Maura.
The next morning
everybody was there.

27

They looked at every goldenrod plant
on the block.

But there were no more golden eggs.

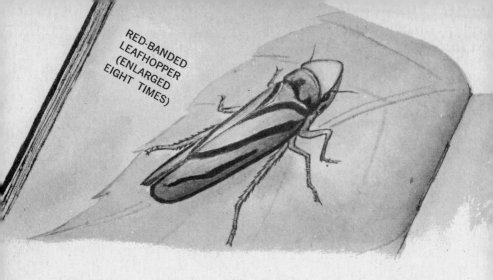

RED-BANDED LEAFHOPPER (ENLARGED EIGHT TIMES)

"There are a lot of little red and blue bugs on the leaves," said Billy.

"Maybe these are the bugs that laid the eggs," said Annie.

"Maybe," said Millie.

At home, she looked up the red and blue insect in the guide.

There it was! On page 34.

It was a red-banded leafhopper.

She saw the children later that day.

She told them the name

of the red and blue insect.

Then she said, "How can we find out

if this is the one that laid the eggs?"

"Let's catch some and put them in jars

with goldenrod leaves," said Becky.

"Maybe they will lay more eggs."

"Let's bug hunt tomorrow," said Nina.

"I'll bring a butterfly net,"

said Annie.

"And I'll bring some jars," said Millie.

They met the next afternoon.

The sun was hot.

They looked for the red and blue

leafhoppers.

"Here's one," cried Matthew.

He tried to catch it

with a little fishnet

he had brought along.

But the leafhopper jumped off the leaf

before the net got near.

"Here's one," cried Annie.

She tried to catch it

with her butterfly net.

Before she got close,

the leafhopper hopped off.

"I see why they are called leafhoppers,"

said Annie.

"They are always

hopping off the leaves."

"I see one,"

cried Greg.

"Where?" asked Jerry.

"Right here," said Greg.

He pointed to a spot on the leaf.

"That's no bug," said Jerry.

"Look again."

"I see one," cried Greg.

"Where?" asked Jerry.

"Right here," said Greg.

He pointed to a little brown bug.

"That's the wrong bug," said Jerry.

"How can we catch these jumpy bugs?"
asked Becky.

"Let's try with our hands," said Nina.

Becky clapped her hands over a leaf.

"I have one!" she cried. "Bring a jar."

Lisa took a jar to her.

"Tear off the leaves and put them all
in here," said Lisa.

Becky put the leaves in the jar.

But before she could get her hands out,
the leafhopper jumped out.

"Let's try that big jar over there,"
she said, "so I can get my hands out."

Lisa brought over the big jar.

Becky found another leafhopper.

This time she got the leaves

and the leafhopper in.

And she got her hands out fast.

Lisa put the lid on fast.

"We have it this time," they both said.

"Couldn't we try at night?"

asked Annie.

"Maybe the bugs won't be so jumpy."

"All right," said Millie.

"Let's meet tomorrow

at seven o'clock, right after dinner.

Bring jars

and punch some holes in the lids."

"Why do the lids have to have holes?"

asked Billy.

"We want the leafhoppers

to stay alive, don't we?

They have to breathe," said Greg.

The next night

everybody was there at seven.

They walked down the street.

Somebody on the block was playing
a Beatle record.

"That's good bug-hunting music,"
Annie said.

Maybe the music helped.

Maybe the leafhoppers were quieter.

They caught seven leafhoppers.

They put them into the jars
with goldenrod leaves.

"The question is, Will they lay eggs?"
said Jerry.

"There has to be a *she* to lay eggs,"
Greg said.

"That's true," said Millie. "But the
he and *she* insects look alike."

"Well," said Maura, "if we have enough
leafhoppers, some are sure to be *she's*."

The next day Millie put the jars

in the sunlight.

Two days later she looked in the jars.

The leafhoppers were dead.

She called the children and asked,

"Why do you think they died?"

She told them where she put the jars.

"Maybe it was too hot," said Becky.

"Let's look at those leaves
before you throw them out,"
said Matthew.
They emptied one jar at a time.
They looked at every leaf.
There were no eggs.
"I'll catch more leafhoppers
and put them in jars again," said Millie.

"Let's all catch more leafhoppers.

It's fun," said Matthew.

The next day they went hunting again.

Nina had a new trick.

She slowly placed the jar upside down

over a goldenrod plant.

Then she broke off the stem

and put the lid on the jar.

"I caught five leafhoppers!" she cried.

Everybody tried the new trick.

In ten minutes they caught

thirty leafhoppers.

"Now we're getting good at it,"

said Greg.

This time Millie took good care of

the jars with the leafhoppers.

She kept them in a cool place

where they got a little sun each day.

"If these leafhoppers

don't lay the right eggs,

the children are going to be sad,"

she thought to herself.

That week she went to a library where

there were books about insects.

She read about

the red-banded leafhopper.

"The females lay their eggs

in the stems and leaves of plants."

She read it over again.

"Then this can't be the right insect.

The eggs we found were *on* the leaves."

The next day she asked the children,

"Will you be upset if the red-banded

leafhopper is not the insect

that laid the golden eggs?"

"What!" said Annie.

"We did it all for nothing!"

"Was it for nothing?" asked Millie.

"Well, we learned how
to catch leafhoppers.
We just picked on the wrong bug,"
said Matthew.

"I have an idea," said Jerry.

"We can catch all the other bugs
on the goldenrod. I saw brown ones
and other kinds. Then we can put
them in jars."

"And then what?" asked Millie.

"And then wait until they lay eggs,"
said Jerry.

"But it is near the end

of the summer," said Millie.

"Lots of insects do not lay eggs now.

Many live through the fall and winter

and lay eggs in the spring."

"We'll wait until then," said Becky,

"and look for more eggs."

"Why does it have to take so long?

I want to know now," said Billy.

"But scientists can't always

find things out quickly," said Millie.

"Who wants to be a scientist

anyhow!" said Matthew.

"I want to know who laid those eggs.

I don't care how long it takes,"

said Lisa.

"Me too," said Nina.

"Suppose we find some more eggs

in the spring. What then?"

asked Millie.

"This time we'll get fresh eggs

before they hatch.

We'll put them in a jar

and see what comes out of them,"

said Jerry.

"It's the only way we will find out."

"But I'll try

the experts anyway,"

thought Millie.

"I still have those few eggs

on the slide."

When she was in the city, she went

to the natural history museum.

She went to the insect department.

She showed a professor the eggs.

"I can't tell you what insect laid these,"

he said, "but I am sure they are

the eggs of a bug—probably a stinkbug.

You had better see the expert on bugs."

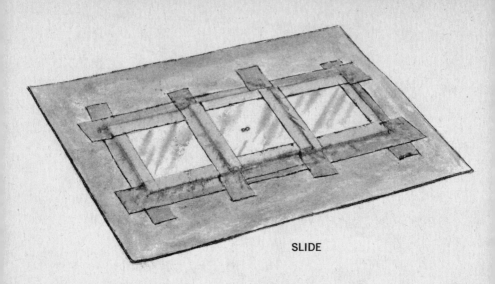

SLIDE

Millie went to the bug expert.

She told him about the children

finding the eggs.

The bug expert looked carefully

at the eggs.

"They look like the eggs of a stinkbug,

but I'm afraid I can't say which one,"

he said. "I'm not an expert on eggs.

Write to Dr. James. Here is his address."

Millie took two of the eggs

and placed them on a new slide.

Then she put the new slide on a card.

She made it stay in place with tape.

"This way it won't break,"

she thought.

Then she wrote a letter to Dr. James.

She asked for the name of the bug

that laid the eggs.

In a week she got a letter.

Dr. James wrote,

"I'm afraid I can't help you.

The eggs were too crushed.

"The only way you can find out

what kind of bug laid these eggs

is to find fresh eggs in the spring.

Let the eggs hatch

and watch the young

bugs grow."

"That's just what the children said,"

thought Millie.

"And that is just what we will do."

Remember:

When you use an insect guide book,

you will find that the word "bug"

does not mean *all* insects

but only one special kind.

A true bug sucks the juices

from plants or animals

through a tube that is formed

by parts of its mouth.

A true bug has front wings that are

thicker at the base.

All bugs are insects—but *not* all

insects are bugs!

Some Books About Insects
You Might Like to Read

Catch a Cricket by Carla Stevens, William R. Scott, New York, 1961.

Caterpillars by Dorothy Sterling, Doubleday, Garden City, New York, 1961.

Collecting Cocoons by Lois J. Hussey and Catherine Pessino, Thomas Y. Crowell, New York, 1953.

Doubleday First Guide To Insects by Su Zan Swain, Doubleday, Garden City, New York, 1964.

First Book of Bugs by Margaret Williamson, Franklin Watts, New York, 1949.

Insects by Robert N. Webb, Whitman, Racine, Wisconsin, 1964.

Insects—A Golden Nature Guide by Herbert S. Zim and Clarence A. Cottam, Golden Press, New York, 1951.

Insects in Their World by Su Zan Swain, Doubleday, Garden City, New York, 1955.